W Blake

CHRISTMAS BOOKS BY THE AUTHOR

Canter, Please!	1935
Important Beginnings	1936
Christmas Greetings	1937
Adventures in Experience	1938
As We Go Galloping On	1939
Vagaries and Verities	1940
In Quest of Oases	1941
A Yuletide Phantasmagoria	1942
Four Years [A Chronicle of World War II]	1943
The Fifth Year [A Further Chronicle of World War II]	1944
Peter Makebelieve	1945
Six Years of Global War	1946
A Journey into Neolithic Times	1947
Isthmus Maximus	1948

OTHER PUBLICATIONS

Behind the Scenes at a Horse Show Charles Scribner's Sons	1948
The Price of Liberty Syracuse University	1948

URIZEN THE CREATOR *[from Europe, a Prophecy]*

BLAKE

THE MYSTIC GENIUS

Adrian Van Sinderen, L.H.D.

1949

SYRACUSE UNIVERSITY PRESS

To
My Wife

*in grateful appreciation
of her co-operation in the
preparation of this book*

CONTENTS

ILLUSTRATIONS

INTRODUCTION

TO the uninitiated the book collector is a benighted being, a hobbyist, victim of an uncontrollable malady which causes him to wander from shop to shop in an admittedly innocent but slightly crazy manner in quest of first editions, unknown manuscripts, and unpublished prints. We collectors tolerate this attitude on the part of our friends in much the same manner that the confirmed horseman smiles at him who has no interest in Man of War or as the incorrigible fisherman regards the man who disdains the fly rod. Men of apparent intelligence have always reveled in their hobbies, and if sometimes they endeavor to convert the Philistine to their pastimes the offense is pardonable.

As a book collector who reverences great books, I have desired for many years to add one more volume to the existing literature concerning William Blake, but a feeling of inadequacy has hitherto prevented the attempt. The embarking upon the venture in no degree lessens that feeling, but serves rather as a reminder that a plunge into icy water always proves the element to be colder even than was imagined. Yet the fact that this book adds its mite to what is already known about Blake certifies it for admission to your shelves the while a certain thrill attends its debut, for in its pages the magnificent series of illustrations of Milton's *L'Allegro* and *Il Penseroso* appear for the first time in colored reproduction. For one hundred thirty years these water-color drawings have lain hidden in the seclusion of closet and safe, protected by the enthusiastic collector from the ravages of time but removed also from the eyes of the multitude.

[13]

It is the proper function of the collector of art or literature to hold in safe-keeping the originals of the world's masterpieces, and the existence today of many items results from his diligence, interest, and acquisitive instinct. An excellent case in point concerns the perpetuation by enthusiasts of the first editions and drawings of William Blake. Only a few copies of his illuminated books survive, partly because his unusual method of printing and coloring the pages entailed so much time and labor that only a few copies were ever completed. It is also true, according to Dr. Geoffrey Keynes in his monumental work, *A Bibliography of William Blake,* 1921, that "the original copper plates [of his illuminated books] have not survived to this day." Blake's original engravings and paintings are equally rare, and even facsimiles tax the purse because of the cost of reproducing his coloring. The only complete edition of Blake's writings has become practically another item for collectors so that the work of Blake, one of England's great poets and one of the world's greatest artists, is not known to the average man of education as is that of Shakespeare or Browning, Reynolds or Gainsborough.

But if the collector is justified in safeguarding such prizes it should be not in the manner of a concealment; rather does the duty fall upon him to share his treasures and when possible assist in their reprinting and reproduction to the end that at least in such secondary form they may be known to the world. In fulfillment of this belief, the author had the privilege in 1924 of furnishing black-and-white copies of the colored plates offered herein to Dr. Geoffrey Keynes of London for inclusion in his splendid two-volume edition of *Milton's Poems* with Blake's illustrations. That masterpiece, published by the Nonesuch Press, 1926, is already a rarity. But black-and-white reproductions never can do justice to the colored originals or adequately substitute for the glories with which the artist endowed the actual work of his hand.

The present volume, in addition to presenting these incomparable pictures to the Blakeian enthusiast, may also serve to induct the tyro to the poetry, philosophy, and creative ability of this mystic genius. If the reader who meets Blake for the first time through these pages is thereby inspired to a further study of his art and thinking this book will serve its purpose.

LIFE

BLAKE'S biography has been well set forth by Alexander Gilchrist in the *Life of William Blake*. My copy is the second edition, London, 1880, too seldom found now in its original blue and gold binding. A summary of the principal facts therein may properly find place here.

Born in 1757, the son of a hosier, Blake lived in London all his life with the exception of four years spent at Felpham. A short man, upright in carriage, he possessed a massive head and wonderful eyes. Like most men of genius he was assertive and dogmatic as to his own beliefs though spiritual and gentle in manner and of great dignity. Following a limited primary education he was apprenticed to an engraver with whom he remained for several years. Such learning as he had came largely from a close study of Milton, Shakespeare, Dante, and the Bible. To these Gibraltars of literature he adhered all his life.

When twenty-five years old he married Catherine Boucher, the daughter of a market gardener, with whom he lived in extreme happiness until his death. She was his companion for almost twenty-four hours of every day, and such education as she acquired derived almost entirely from her husband. He and his wife made their first home in Leicester Fields, moving later to Poland Street, where they resided for five years before transferring in 1793 across Westminster Bridge to Lambeth.

Blake was a prodigious worker throughout his life. As a young man he began to write poetry, first in the more simple form found in the *Songs of Innocence,* later in the complex idiom and prophetic strain of his created mythology. The artist, however, superseded the poet. To write the *Songs* was also to illustrate them, and today Blake's books are desired more for the illustrations than for the text.

It is the object of art to enrich the soul through the eye by presenting in shape and color the realities of hope, strength, motion, the elements, and the naked human body. Blake magnificently portrayed these things, but on the other hand he failed to understand the grace and charm of color of the art of his own day, and much of its beauty seems to have been lost to him. This fact accounts for his hostility to Sir Joshua Reynolds and for his *Annotations to Reynolds' Discourses*, wherein he censures the great portrait painter; jealousy may also have played its part, for Blake was an unknown artist and Reynolds the famous President of the Royal Academy. This fact and his hostility to neoclassical artistic theory account for his antagonism to Reynolds.

Blake did not travel, had no circle of important friends such as gathered around Dr. Johnson, and possessed not the means to belong to clubs or to become a sportsman; therefore the story of his life lacks the usual run of anecdotes which associate themselves with great or politically prominent men. Assiduous and unceasing work both as author and artist filled his every day. The authoritative writings of Gilchrist, Damon, Binyon, and Swinburne furnish the details of his seventy years of labor and prove pleasant reading when found, for even these biographies do not appear on every book shelf.

On August 12, 1827, Blake died in his seventieth year; his body lies buried at Bunhill Fields Burying Ground, but no one of the several hundred headstones there refers to its final resting place. As in the case of so many of the world's great masters, fame came to Blake posthumously, for he derived but small recompense from his arduous labors. He spent his last years in a two-room apartment which served his wife and himself both as dwelling place and workshop. Despite the lack of recognition, despite poverty, without a formal education or a chance to see the world, Blake proved again the truth that inadequate opportunities and scanty means cannot defeat a genius.

ART

WHO was this Blake who lived so inconspicuously in England's capital? What did he produce? What heritage has he left to the world? Let us attempt to answer these questions.

To begin with, Blake was a mystic. This thought must remain uppermost at all times in studying him, and to understand Blake requires serious study. His genius found its greatest realization in portraying the human soul and this he attempted to do both in his art and in his writings. One difficulty in endeavoring to reach an understanding of Blake lies in the fact that he cannot be summarized. He was a bold man, pure in heart. He unhesitatingly looked truth in the eye as many men dare not do, and he developed a philosophy which succeeding generations have not had the courage to accept in its entirety. Although Blake has been dead for nearly a century and a quarter, we still somewhat fear him, and we still do not entirely fathom his mysticism nor completely comprehend his symbolism. Recent books about Blake emphasize that his work was an interpretation of his personal life, and this approach may give us a more complete picture of the man.

Blake possessed great literary power and great pictorial power. Seldom are both found in one man. As he was an imaginative writer so too was he an imaginative artist. It might seem that the art and writings of Blake would lend themselves to separate study but such is not the case, for the reason that both express his philosophy. We must approach him through the medium of his art at the same time that we study his writings. ·

Drawn by W. Blake.   Etched by L. Schiavonetti

As we have said, Blake wrote about the human soul. He did not attempt descriptive poetry nor did he paint objects which he physically saw. It would have been completely foreign to him to commemorate an actual event in writing or to place upon canvas or upon bronze plate a landscape or a portrait. Instead of portraying living models, he chose to depict images of the mind, and he found no difficulty in presenting Free Will, Good or Evil, Clouds or Stars as individuals. In thus personifying an idea, Blake had of necessity to express his meaning in abstract impersonations. Therefore, his figures possess little individuality in their faces. He regarded the human soul as a personified reality and visualized God as a distinct person.

Blake enjoyed a purposeful life, centered on the endeavor to open the eyes of men to truth as he saw it, and he conveyed his message not by preaching but through the mediums of his writing and his drawings. A concept of the enormous quantity of his verse and prose may be quickly gained from the complete listing which appears in *The Writings of William Blake*, 1925, edited by Dr. Geoffrey Keynes. A partial list of his books appears in the present volume. To glimpse readily the vast treasure of designs which he bequeathed to posterity presents a more difficult task, for no one book includes his entire output. Oil paintings were not his forte but his many water-colors, drawings, and engravings rank among the finest in art. As already stated, he invented his own secret method of printing and coloring his illuminated books, and the fact that such personal labor could produce only a few copies did not deter him from employing it. Only three of his books were originally printed in ordinary typography, *Poetical Sketches*, 1787, *The French Revolution*, 1791, one copy only, and *A Descriptive Catalogue*, which details the exhibition of his pictures held in 1809.

Blake studied Gothic architecture intently and its style so greatly influenced his ideas that his fundamental reliance upon the adequacy of form and line sometimes resulted in an inadequacy in his shadings. It is not our function to enter here into a detailed analysis of Blake's art but the student who so desires will find authoritative comment on the subject; he will naturally wish to view not only those designs which are found in Blake's own books but also that great quantity of material contained in some sixty other books which he illustrated. Throughout his life, a steady stream of single drawings and engravings to ennoble the works of other authors flowed from his workroom, and today no competent collection of Blake is without examples of these masterpieces, either the original or in facsimile. Dr. Keynes' *A Bibliography of William Blake,* 1921, lists this material in orderly fashion. In some books such as *The Complaint, and the Consolation: or Night Thoughts,* by Edward Young, generally known as Young's *Night Thoughts,* the illustrations are entirely marginal, a favorite form with Blake. On the other hand, full-page pictures in *The Grave* by Robert Blair embody the artist's philosophy. The plate which here appears, entitled THE SOUL HOVERING OVER THE BODY RELUCTANTLY PARTING WITH LIFE, illustrates better than any words Blake's conception of the union between soul and body.

It was on Blake's return from Felpham to London in 1803 that R. H. Cromek, a publisher, employed him to do the drawings for *The Grave.* Blake expected to do both the designing and the engraving of the plates but Cromek, who exploited Blake, took the twenty designs and turned them over to a well-known engraver named Schiavonetti, at whose hands twelve plates found place in the book, which became a popular seller. Gilchrist recounts at length Blake's difficulties with Cromek.

Mention should also be made of the plates illustrating *Paradise Lost, Comus,* and *Dante.* While the original editions are so rare as to be seen only in great libraries, a number of reproductions exist. The finding of one on a bookseller's shelf will make a day memorable and whet the appetite of the proud purchaser to a renewed seeking for these veritable treasures.

During his last thirty years, Blake was blessed with two patron friends without whom his life of poverty would have been even more difficult. Thomas Butts so constantly purchased Blake's works that his own house became almost a Blake museum; indeed Butts first bought the colored drawings herein included. With Butts' assistance, Blake, at the age of sixty-six, entered upon the creation of the twenty-one INVENTIONS, as he called them, for the *Book of Job,* the noblest work to come from his hand. Upon their completion,

THEN A SPIRIT PASSED BEFORE MY FACE *[from Book of Job]*

Shall mortal Man be more Just than God? Shall a Man be more Pure than his Maker? Behold he putteth no trust in his Saints & his Angels he chargeth with folly

WBlake invenit & sculp

Then a Spirit passed before my face
the hair of my flesh stood up

London. Published as the Act directs March 8: 1825 by William Blake N 3 Fountain Court, Strand

Proof

WHEN THE MORNING STARS SANG TOGETHER *[from Book of Job]*

14

Canst thou bind the sweet influences of Pleiades or loose the bands of Orion

Let there Be

Light

And God made Two Great Lights

Sun

Noon

Let there be. A

Firmament

Let the Waters bring forth abundantly

Let the Waters be gathered together into one place

& let the Dry Land appear

Let the Earth bring forth

Cattle & Creeping thing & Beast

When the morning Stars sang together, & all the Sons of God shouted for joy

W Blake Inverit & Sc

London. Published as the Act directs March 8. 1825 by Will Blake N.3 Fountain Court Strand.

Proof

his friend and patron, John Linnell, paid him fairly handsomely to produce another set; the drawings made for Linnell surpass those designed for Butts. The INVENTIONS to the *Book of Job* have been considered as representing Blake's finest work and it is fitting to include here two plates from this series. The first, THEN A SPIRIT PASSED BEFORE MY FACE, exemplifies the true Blakeian style; the second, WHEN THE MORNING STARS SANG TOGETHER, has been acclaimed his greatest conception. This plate has meaning as well as beauty, for it presents a sort of map of the universe. Below is the world of flesh; at the left center is shown the world of the intellect, while the right center represents the realm of emotions. At the top is the world of the spirit, while in the center, binding all together, is God, the Divine Imagination.

The great artist passed his final years in the execution of one hundred drawings, of which only seven were engraved, designed as illustrations for Dante's *Divine Comedy*. The book is dated 1827.

PHILOSOPHY

WE speak often of freedom; the attempt to gain it has concerned every phase of man's existence. The realms of faith, love, action, thought, have all been the scenes of frightful conflict in man's effort to gain freedom. The progress of civilization may be traced by measuring the quantity of freedom which the human race has won from its beginnings until a given time. But man has discovered that even freedom requires the restraining influences of law, and he has endeavored to discover those fundamental principles of faith, of family life, of action, which will place necessary limits upon unbridled liberty.

To Blake, the philosopher, such thinking was anathema. He contended that laws stultify the power to create and constrict by their inescapable rigidity. He believed that the way to truth, the way to God, lies in the imagination, and that only by complete freedom can man reach his highest powers of imagination. On the other hand, he felt that not every man merited this freedom because some are too weak to understand such a philosophy. In his own words: "Those who restrain desire do so because their own desire is weak enough to be restrained."

Again and again did Blake object to any restriction which prevents man from reaching the highest flights of imagination, and he voices his contention in an immortal sentence: "What is now proved was once only imagined." He was also supremely interested, says Swinburne, "in the strife, which never can be ended, between the imagination which apprehends the spirit of a thing and that approach which dissects the body of a fact."

A major factor in Blake's philosophy was the influence of Emanuel Sweden-borg, a mystic, who wrote a book entitled *Heaven and Hell,* its title closely akin to Blake's *The Marriage of Heaven and Hell.*

Blake's prophetic books expound the theory that tyranny constantly over-whelms freedom and that revolution follows the reign of tyranny. This view-point carried to its ultimate conclusion forced him to become a close thinker regarding every phase of man's existence, and he applied his opposition to restraint to the physical, the mental, and the spiritual life. For this reason, although a devout believer in God and very definitely a Christian, he op-posed many acts of the Church, which he felt resulted in restraint of man.

Blake constantly emphasized his insistence that body and soul are one and often restated this thought. The following quotations evidence that other authors have agreed with him:

SPENSER: For of the soule the bodie forme doth take:
                For soule is forme, and doth the body make.
SHELLEY: Soul is the only element.
WHITMAN: I have said that the soul is not more than the body
                And I have said that the body is not more than the soul.

His philosophy brought him face to face with the matter of sex. It appears that Blake's highest imagination was stirred by what we may term sexual art. Believing that everything that lives is holy, and that man's body is not distinct from his soul, he proceeded to the view that a man's highest develop-ment requires a perfect love. Perhaps, I can best explain his view by saying that Blake believed every man entitled to an ideal union because such a union has an utterly sacred meaning. If marriage, a law-given union, did not result in the perfect state Blake thought that a man should not be con-strained by its restriction. His attitude toward sex reflected not amorous lust but the essentiality of the highest ideal. He knew that man's deepest instinct is rooted in sex, and he regarded wedlock as extending into eternity. Blake was among the first to write of sex as a holy thing; the literature of his century voiced quite another note.

[28]

"Blake's sex theory," writes Damon, "is generally misunderstood," and Swinburne states that to Blake "not pleasure, but hypocrisy, is the unclean thing."

The holding of this tenet and the fact that Blake neither defended chastity nor advocated license has resulted in the criticism that he was a protagonist of "free love." My reading of him does not confirm this thought in the ordinary use of these words. I think that Blake found a vast difference between love that is free and "free love"; he demanded single, ideal realization of the finest in life but not promiscuity. While he went so far as to advocate the consummation of an ideal love, he himself found complete happiness with his own mate; there is no evidence that he indulged in illicit practise.

This philosophy forms the burden of the message of the *Visions of the Daughters of Albion,* a lament on the condition of love in the world. In it the author points out that love that is free is the highest ideal but impractical. In this poem the author emphasized that conventional restraints arising from sexual jealousy poison love.

Further development of Blake's philosophy occurs in *The Marriage of Heaven and Hell,* of which Swinburne wrote, "A work which we rank about the greatest product of the eighteenth century in the line of high poetry and spiritual speculation. Here he has written a book as perfect as his most faultless song. His fire of spirit fills it from end to end. The variety and audacity of thoughts and words are incomprehensible. One of his *Proverbs of Hell* might serve as the motto of the book, 'No bird soars too high if he soars on his own wings.'"

The Marriage sets forth as an important cornerstone of Blake's philosophy, that all opposites form parts of an overall unification. He believed that attraction and repulsion, reason and energy, love and hate are all necessary to human existence. He developed this idea into the reasoning that from these various opposites come those forces which religion divides into Good and Evil, reasoning which he found to be confused. He carried this unification of opposites to the ultimate, and throughout his books runs the theme that all things exist in eternity rather than in the present. His writings frequently

[29]

state that the contrasting of Heaven and Hell, God and Satan, and other accepted opposites are ideas which exist only by man's invention. Such thinking deserves careful consideration.

While Blake's ideals of morality outrage some readers, his greatest biographer has termed *The Marriage of Heaven and Hell* the most daring and courageous of Blake's works. That the poetry itself is not easy reading may be inferred from the opening lines which are typical of the author's style:

> "Rintrah roars and shakes his fires in the burden'd air;
>   Hungry clouds swag on the deep."*

In this book the author voices his philosophy in certain sentences headed *The Voice of the Devil:*

"All Bibles or sacred codes have been the causes of the following Errors:
1. That Man has two real existing principles: Viz: a Body & a Soul.
2. That Energy, call'd Evil, is alone from the Body; & that Reason call'd Good, is alone from the Soul.
3. That God will torment Man in Eternity for following his Energies."

"But the following Contraries to these are True:
1. Man has no Body distinct from his Soul; for that call'd Body is a portion of Soul discern'd by the five Senses, the chief inlets of Soul in this age.
2. Energy is the only life, and is from the Body; and Reason is the bound or outward circumference of Energy."

These observations reveal that Blake developed an idea with precision and followed it through to its logical conclusion.

Another section of the book, entitled *Proverbs of Hell,* includes these lines:
"Prudence is a rich ugly old maid courted by Incapacity."
"Prisons are built with stones of Law, Brothels with bricks of Religion."
"The fox condemns the trap, not himself."
"To create a little flower is the work of the ages."
"You never know what is enough unless you know what is more than enough."

---

*Note: Rintrah personifies the wrath of the Honest Man.

Always he refused to believe in any philosophy based merely upon accepted phrase or conventional approach. His *Annotations to Reynolds' Discourses to the Royal Academy* further evidence his forthright analysis of the pronouncements of authority with whom he disagreed.

REYNOLDS: He was a great generalizer…But this disposition to abstractions, to generalizing and classification, is the great glory of the human mind.
BLAKE: To generalize is to be an idiot. To particularize is the alone distinction of merit. General knowledges are those knowledges that idiots possess.

REYNOLDS: Such was his love of his art, and such his ardour to excel, that he often declared he had, during the greater part of his life, laboured as hard with his pencil, as any mechanick working at his trade for bread.
BLAKE: The man who does not labour more than the hireling must be a poor devil.

REYNOLDS: Most people err, not so much from want of capacity to find their object, as from not knowing what object to pursue.
BLAKE: The man who does not know what object to pursue is an idiot.

REYNOLDS: The errors of genius…are pardonable.
BLAKE: Genius has no error; it is ignorance that is error.

BLAKE: Gainsborough told a gentleman of rank and fortune that the worst painters always chose the grandest subjects. I desired the gentleman to set Gainsborough about one of Rafael's grandest subjects, namely, Christ delivering the keys to St. Peter, and he would find that in Gainsborough's hands it would be a vulgar subject of a poor fisherman and a journeyman carpenter.

REYNOLDS: In the midst of the highest flights of fancy or imagination, reason ought to preside from first to last.
BLAKE: If this is true, it is devilish foolish thing to be an artist.

Another example of his insistence on the validity of his own thinking even when opposed by authority is found in his expression of antipathy to certain tenets of Sir Francis Bacon. Keynes and Gilchrist both record the existence of a copy of the *Essays* which Blake once owned and annotated. This particular copy may no longer exist, for Keynes in his *Bibliography* makes the following reference to it:

"This copy was seen by Gilchrist but it has not been consulted by any other authority. I have been informed that it was in the possession of Mr. Lionel Isaacs of the Haymarket about 1900 but I have not been able to trace it any further."

The biographer Gilchrist must have seen this book for he states that it is replete with Blake's adverse criticism of Bacon, most of it unreasonable. Blake's philosophy concerning brotherly love and justice to all mankind finds expression therein, however, in at least one annotation with which modern thinking will agree.

Bacon wrote:

"The increase of any State must be upon the foreigner."

To this Blake commented:

"The increase of a State as of a man, is from internal improvement or intellectual acquirement. Man is not improved by the hurt of another nor is a State improved at the expense of foreigners."

To read about Blake, however, is like reading about the Bible or Shakespeare; the only way to grasp the philosophy expressed in great books is to read the books themselves.

WRITINGS

A critical commentary anent the poetry, the philosophy and the prophetic mysticism of Blake would comfortably fill an entire volume and therefore the attempt to analyze Blake's writings within the confines of one chapter evidences perhaps a greater temerity than wisdom. The limited space of this exposition will at least suffice to set in array the salient features of the poet's literary compositions.

We may include first as a group those minor works which number among others *The Poetical Sketches,* 1787; *There Is No Natural Religion,* 1789; *Tiriel,* 1789; *The French Revolution,* 1791; and *A Descriptive Catalogue,* 1809. Three of these works were printed in ordinary typography, the only ones thus produced, for early in his life Blake began to publish his illuminated books. *There Is No Natural Religion* belongs to this latter category while *Tiriel* exists in manuscript only, except for reprintings.

The author's first immortal book was *Songs of Innocence,* 1789. This, one of his highest poetic achievements, was followed in 1794 by a companion volume *Songs of Innocence and Experience,* which bears the subtitle *Showing the Two Contrary States of the Human Soul.* The tenderness of these poems sets them apart from all of Blake's subsequent writings. In them, his best known verse, Blake expresses not the author's but a child's happiness. It is a child who speaks through the lines.

These volumes, executed by the method of illuminated printing which was to serve the author for all his later books, are perhaps the favorite items of collectors of Blake's works. In most copies the plates are printed in brown although some appear in green or blue ink. In each case the verse and the design, or illustration, were both outlined on a copper plate, from which the impression was made in the ground color desired. The page was then colored by hand.

SONGS OF INNOCENCE

Piping down the valleys wild,
Piping songs of pleasant glee,
On a cloud I saw a child,
And he laughing said to me:

"Pipe a song about a Lamb!"
So I piped with merry chear.
"Piper, pipe that song again;"
So I piped: he wept to hear.

"Drop thy pipe, thy happy pipe;
"Sing thy songs of happy chear:"
So I sung the same again,
While he wept with joy to hear.

"Piper, sit thee down and write
"In a book, that all may read."
So he vanish'd from my sight,
And I pluck'd a hollow reed,

And I made a rural pen,
And I stain'd the water clear,
And I wrote my happy songs
Every child may joy to hear.

THE LAMB

Little Lamb, who made thee?
Dost thou know who made thee?
Gave thee life, & bid thee feed
By the stream & o'er the mead;
Gave thee clothing of delight,
Softest clothing, wooly, bright;
Gave thee such a tender voice,
Making all the vales rejoice?
　　Little Lamb, who made thee?
　　Dost thou know who made thee?

Little Lamb, I'll tell thee,
Little Lamb, I'll tell thee:
He is called by thy name,
For he calls himself a Lamb.
He is meek, & he is mild,
He became a little child.
I a child, & thou a lamb,
We are called by his name.
　　Little Lamb, God bless thee!
　　Little Lamb, God bless thee!

Could any pen inscribe more beautiful or more compassionate words than
those of *The Divine Image?*

THE DIVINE IMAGE

To Mercy, Pity, Peace, and Love
　　All pray in their distress;
And to these virtues of delight
　　Return their thankfulness.

For Mercy, Pity, Peace, and Love
   Is God, our Father dear;
And Mercy, Pity, Peace, and Love,
   Is Man, his child and care.

For Mercy has a human heart,
   Pity a human face,
And Love, the human form divine,
   And Peace, the human dress.

Then every man, of every clime,
   That prays in his distress,
Prays to the human form divine,
   Love, Mercy, Pity, Peace.

And all must love the human form,
   In heathen, turk, or jew;
Where Mercy, Love, & Pity dwell
   There God is dwelling too.

In his famous poem, *The Tyger,* which appears in *Songs of Experience,* Blake makes a contrast with *The Lamb,* from *Songs of Innocence,* and raises the question as to how God who made the lamb could bring himself to make anything so deadly and strong as the tiger. *The Tyger* is a symbolic poem in which the "forests of the night" are the stars in the heavens; the "immortal hand or eye" is the Creator. "Distant deeps or skies" suggests chaos before the creation of the world. The hammer, chain, and furnace form part of creation not only in this poem but in other of Blake's works. *The Tyger* may be interpreted symbolically and it asks a question which even Blake did not answer when he queries

   "Did he smile his work to see?
   Did he who made the Lamb make thee?"

THE TYGER

Tyger! Tyger! burning bright
In the forests of the night,
What immortal hand or eye
Could frame thy fearful symmetry?

In what distant deeps or skies
Burnt the fire of thine eyes?
On what wings dare he aspire?
What the hand dare seize the fire?

And what shoulder, & what art,
Could twist the sinews of thy heart?
And when thy heart began to beat,
What dread hand? & what dread feet?

What the hammer? what the chain?
In what furnace was thy brain?
What the anvil? what dread grasp
Dare its deadly terrors clasp?

When the stars threw down their spears,
And water'd heaven with their tears,
Did he smile his work to see?
Did he who made the Lamb make thee?

Tyger! Tyger! burning bright
In the forests of the night,
What immortal hand or eye
Dare frame thy fearful symmetry?

The Book of Thel, 1789, a purely Blakeian product, followed the *Songs of Innocence.* The story portrays the unborn spirit of a woman, Thel, who seeks the reason for life. This unborn spirit receives advice on the subject from four characters portrayed as the Lily of the Valley, the Cloud, the Worm, and the Clod of Clay, representing respectively infancy, youth, adolescence, and maturity. The Clod of Clay, or maturity, invites Thel to earth, a figurative way of suggesting the metamorphosis of an unborn spirit into life through a mother. Thel finds the sorrows of earth so discouraging that she rushes back to the happiness of eternity.

In 1790, appeared *The Marriage of Heaven and Hell,* which we considered in a previous chapter, and then in 1793 a sequel to *The Book of Thel* entitled the *Visions of the Daughters of Albion.* In this book, the heroine Thel, who appears under the name of Oothoon, is in love with Theotormon, who represents the emotional side of life, but is violated by Bromion, who represents the rational side of life. The book contains 11 plates of illuminated printing. Keynes cites that thirteen copies exist.

Following the *Visions of the Daughters of Albion,* Blake began to write the prophetic books. As he found no existing prototypes to represent the forces which he desired to feature, he created personages to fill these roles. Throughout these books a number of such characters appear, but we have space here to describe only the chief actors of the dramas.

Los, who represents the poetic instinct, is the ruler of Time. His wife, or Emanation, named Enitharmon, is the ruler of Space. Urizen (in other words, your reason) is the God of Reason. Blake argues that Urizen, or Reason, has always tried to rule the world, but constantly destroys it because of the tyranny of his laws. Blake found that man falsely worships Urizen, instead of allowing his imagination free play. Orc, or the spirit of revolt, typifies the spirit of youth which Blake thought of as the heart. Hence "cor" or heart becomes transposed into Orc. Albion represents universal man. The student who desires to make an intensive study of Blake's mythology and the meaning of his mysticism should consult that masterful exposition of the subject by S. Foster Damon, *William Blake, his Philosophy and Symbols.*

The first prophetic book is titled *America, A Prophecy*, 1793. In the American Revolution, Blake saw the hope of a foreshadowed freedom of all mankind. *America* does not follow the details of the war, but certain well-known persons appear including George Washington and Benjamin Franklin. However, the chief characters in the book are the mythological creations of Blake's mind. Revolt appears in the person of Orc, and the Prince of Albion personifies Oppression.

The prophetic strain continues in the next book, *Europe, A Prophecy*, 1794, which covers the period of the Christian era from the birth of Christ until the time of Blake. Two known copies contain all of the 18 magnificent plates, one of which, known sometimes as THE ANCIENT OF DAYS and sometimes as URIZEN, THE CREATOR, appears as the frontispiece of the present volume. The plate shows Urizen, the God of Reason, measuring out the world with a compass, a thought which may derive from the sentence in the *Book of Proverbs*: "He set a compass upon the face of the deep." The book introduces Enitharmon, Los, and Orc. The text is confused in meaning.

While still in Lambeth, Blake continued his prophetic writing with *The First Book of Urizen*, 1794, *The Book of Ahania*, 1795, *The Book of Los*, 1795, and *The Song of Los*, 1795. Mr. Damon writes: "*The Book of Los* ends with the creation of Adam; *The First Book of Urizen* deals with the first civilization in Egypt; *Ahania* ends with the rise of Asia." *The Song of Los* continues the story of these books, all of them difficult to comprehend and filled with bewildering symbolism.

An excellent commentary on *Urizen* by Dorothy Plowman appears in the facsimile edition published by J. M. Dent & Sons, London, 1929. The story tells how Urizen was exiled into Chaos as a result of enslaving mankind in a material and finite world. It was Blake's thought that reason is responsible for evil through the creation of ethical codes and through making infinity finite and eternity mortal. Twenty-eight magnificent plates in brilliant color constitute this series, but the book will never arouse popular interest because of its note of despair. Two of the finest plates portray Urizen in chains and Urizen in Chaos. Seven copies of the book are known.

Blake thought of titling his next work, "The Second Book of Urizen," but later changed to *The Book of Ahania*. Its pages, probably devoid of illustrations except for two vignettes, depict the flight of Israel from Egypt, the giving of the law of Moses, and the settlement in Asia. Ahania herself, the emanation of Urizen, represents pleasure.

The Book of Los is a brief work of confused symbolism; Blake printed only one complete copy which is now in the British Museum.

The Song of Los deals with the story of man from the beginning of civilization to the American Revolution and records the founding of various religious creeds which Urizen, or Reason, has given to man under the guise of mythology. It contains eight brilliant plates which reveal Blake as a great designer and colorist.

Fortunately, the manuscript of Blake's greatest prophetic book, *The Four Zoas*, 1804, has survived and rests now in the British Museum. The first form of the title was *"Vala, The Death and Judgment of the Ancient Man: A Dream of Nine Nights."* This division of the book, he adopted in place of chapters. Vala personifies nature. The Zoas represent the spirit, the head, the heart, and the loins, impersonated by the mythical characters Urthona, Urizen, Luvah, and Tharmas; the author sets forth that in the beginning these Zoas existed in one man, Albion. The story takes place in the times before the opening of the *Book of Genesis* and relates that men try to govern their lives by reason only to find that reason is insufficient authority because it cannot govern instinct. Those who would undertake further study of this book are referred to Max Plowman's *Introduction to the Study of Blake* which contains a chapter on *The Four Zoas*.

In 1800, Blake accepted the invitation of William Hayley to move to Felpham and while there wrote the greater part of two books, *Jerusalem, The Emanation of the Giant Albion*, published in 1820, and *Milton, A Poem*, published in 1808. *Jerusalem*, a complex work in which the mythology is further complicated by the addition of new characters, contains illustrations in Blake's usual style and the mystical text has further pronouncements of the author's philosophy. Particular emphasis is placed on forgiveness.

"All things exist in the human imagination."

"And this is the manner of the sons of Albion in their strength:
  They take the Two Contraries which are call'd Qualities, with which
  Every Substance is clothed: they name them Good & Evil."

"He who would do good to another, must do it in minute particulars:
  General good is the plea of the scoundrel, hypocrite, and flatterer."

"It is easier to forgive an enemy than to forgive a friend."

"I heard His voice in my sleep, and His angel in my dream
  Saying, Doth Jehovah forgive a debt, only on condition that it shall
  Be paid? Doth He forgive pollution only on condition of purity?
  That debt is not forgiven! That pollution is not forgiven!
  Such is the forgiveness of the gods; the moral virtues of the
  Heathen, whose tender mercies are cruelty. But Jehovah's salvation
  Is without money and without price, in the continual forgiveness of sins."

Blake's *Milton*, which carries the subtitle *To Justify the Ways of God to Man*, was finished in 1804 but not published until 1808. In this story John Milton comes back to earth and enters into the body of William Blake, his return being due to the fact that he believes that in writing *Paradise Lost* he upheld in error both materialism and morals. Feeling that he had thus erred he endeavors to correct the wrong. The book, richly illustrated with colored plates, offers a confused, complex, and not understandable piece of writing. One copy exists with a total of 50 plates, the drawings majestic and well composed. Mr. Damon has written that, "as literature *Milton* has the simplest plan of all Blake's long works," but the reader should not infer from this statement that he is in for easy reading in attempting to understand this poem.

For many years, Blake kept a notebook in which he drew sketches for future etchings and entered the first drafts of some of his poems. After his death his wife gave the book to one of his pupils, Samuel Palmer, whose brother sold it for a few shillings to Dante Gabriel Rossetti. This little volume, which has come to be known as the *Rossetti Manuscript*, constitutes a revered Blake item. It appeared in facsimile reproduction in 1935 from the Nonesuch Press. In it most of the illustrations of *The Gates of Paradise* and many of those for Blake's other books find place. Among its nuggets occurs the following:

ETERNITY

He who bends to himself a joy
Does the wingèd life destroy;
But he who kisses the joy as it flies
Lives in eternity's sunrise.

While at Felpham, Blake wrote the lyrics which make up what is now known as the *Pickering Manuscript,* dated 1801-1803.

AUGURIES OF INNOCENCE

To see a World in a Grain of Sand
And a Heaven in a Wild Flower,
Hold Infinity in the palm of your hand,
And Eternity in an hour.

Each outcry of the hunted Hare
A fibre from the Brain does tear.
A Skylark wounded in the wing,
A Cherubim does cease to sing.

After returning to London from Felpham, Blake made the illustrations for *The Gates of Paradise.* When first issued the title had the prefix "For Children" by which Blake meant that it was for those whose vision was undimmed. Later, he became discouraged with the restricted thinking of his readers and changed it to read "For the Sexes," to wit, those who live in a generative world. A rare original contains twenty-one plates. Two of the most significant

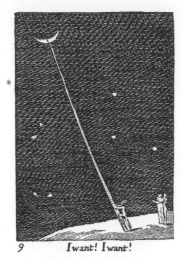

9   I want! I want!   10   Help! Help!

Publishd by WBlake 17 May 1793

are here included. I WANT! I WANT! shows youth reaching for the moon while two lovers look on. The plate, HELP! HELP! portrays man drowning in a sea of realism.

A short commentary and an epilogue furnish the text, but the plates can best be enjoyed for themselves alone. Through them we see Blake impatient of man's stupidness and angry at the thought that we humans do not progressively develop throughout life. He embodies his philosophy in the opening lines:

> Mutual Forgiveness of each Vice,
> Such are the Gates of Paradise.
>
> Jehovah's fingers wrote The Law:
> Then wept! then rose in Zeal & Awe,
> And in the midst of Sinai's heat
> Hid it beneath his Mercy Seat.
> O Christians, Christians! tell me Why
> You rear it on your Altars high!

[43]

As we have already said, Blake cannot be summarized. Those who have chronicled his life have suggested that he was mentally unstable. *"Nullum magnum ingenium sine mixtura dementiae fuit."* So Seneca in his *"De Tranquilitate Animi"* quoted Aristotle when he wrote that there never was a great genius without a tincture of madness. Perhaps, compared with the mold of the man of reason, Blake had a tincture of madness. But if so, this judgment must apply to others of the world's greatest creators who have found truth through a God-inspired imagination, an imagination which created beauty and which visioned horizons beyond the sight of those who see only with their eyes. Perhaps such imagination played a part in Sibelius' music. Perhaps Wagner and Shelley were mad, as some of their contemporaries argued. I give thanks for the *Second Symphony, Die Götterdämmerung,* the ode *To a Skylark,* and also for Blake's visions. We need that kind of madness or purity of thought which realizes that "All things exist in the human imagination," and that "What is now proved was once only imagined." Blake's imaginings are windows which have let in upon this earth a new light from eternity.

PROVENANCE

WE come now to the Illustrations to *L'Allegro* and *Il Penseroso* which occasion the writing of this book. These designs received their first authoritative mention in Gilchrist's *Life and Works of William Blake*. The second edition, Volume II, page 246, states:

"Twelve illustrations to the 'Allegro' and 'Penseroso.' (Butts)"

"A very pretty and interesting series in which Blake's turn for personifying and idealising comes out as strong as in 'Prophetic Books,' but divested of terror, and, of course, following the main lines traced by the poet. Each design is accompanied by a slip of Blake's handwriting, giving the extract from the poem and his own analysis of the design."

Laurence Binyon in his introduction to the reproduction of the *Book of Job,* 1906, evidences his knowledge of the existence of these drawings by this reference on page 57:

"So in his designs to Milton's *Penseroso* he introduces the sun 'flinging his flaring beams' as an actual human figure darting javelins."

A Bibliography of William Blake, Geoffrey Keynes, New York, 1921, refers to the series on page 416 in connection with the Earl of Crewe's sale in 1903.

The next mention occurs in *The Writings of William Blake,* edited by Dr. Keynes, 1925. Volume III, page 408 has this statement:

"This series of illustrations has never been reproduced and is very little known at the present time. Each design is accompanied by Blake's transcript of the lines illustrated, together with his own brief description of the picture. The series is in the possession of Mr. Adrian Van Sinderen."

In 1926, the Nonesuch Press printed *Milton's Poems* with Blake's illustrations and on page 271 appears the following:

"A number of Blake's designs have never been reproduced in any form. This applies more particularly to the series illustrating *L'Allegro* and *Il Penseroso;* these could not have been included even now without the courteous cooperation of Mr. Adrian Van Sinderen of New York, and to him are due the thanks of the publisher, editor and the discriminating public."

The reproductions referred to are in black and white. Page 274 of the same book contains this additional data:

"The twelve designs are water-colour drawings measuring about 16 x 12 cms. They are signed by Blake, but not dated, and were included by W. M. Rossetti in his list of undated works. They are, however, executed upon Whatman paper with the date 1816 in the watermark, and must belong either to that year or the next, for Blake is very unlikely to have bought more than a small quantity of expensive drawing paper at any one time. The drawings are probably, therefore, the last of the Milton series. They have been mounted in a folio volume bound in russian leather. With each picture is a leaf about 17 x 11 cms. giving in Blake's hand the lines which it illustrates, together with a brief description in his own words."

"This series was formerly in the collection of Thomas Butts and must have been among the last works which he bought from Blake. It was no doubt afterwards acquired from Butts's son by Richard Monckton Milnes, first Lord Houghton, and so came into the possession of the Earl of Crewe with whose collection it was sold at Sotheby's on March 30, 1903. It was then taken to America."

The drawings became the property of Mr. Alfred T. White of Brooklyn, New York, and on his death in 1921 were inherited by his daughter, Mrs. Adrian Van Sinderen.

A final mention of them occurs in the catalogue of the Philadelphia Museum of Art, 1939:

"It is a singularly interesting series of pictures, not only for the beauty of the bright, light and many-tinted coloring, but because it affords an unusual opportunity to understand Blake's interpretation of the poetry. They rank among his finest paintings."

The careful reader will desire to focus his attention upon every detail of these paintings if he is fully to comprehend their meaning. Each one is a pictorial translation of certain lines of the poem as understood by the artist. Each plate will reveal beauty even to the casual observer but one must gaze long and earnestly desire to discover the majesty, the mysticism and the power with which this series is endowed.

L'ALLEGRO

by John Milton

HENCE loathèd Melancholy,
   Of Cerberus and blackest Midnight born,
   In Stygian Cave forlorn
  'Mongst horrid shapes, and shrieks, and sights unholy!
Find out some uncouth cell,
   Where brooding Darkness spreads his jealous wings,
And the night-Raven sings;
   There under Ebon shades, and low-browed Rocks,
As ragged as thy Locks,
   In dark Cimmerian desert ever dwell.
But come, thou Goddess fair and free,
In Heaven yclept Euphrosyne,
And by men, heart-easing Mirth,
Whom lovely Venus, at a birth,
With two sister Graces more,
To Ivy-crownèd Bacchus bore;
Or whether (as some Sager sing)
The Frolic Wind that breathes the Spring,
Zephir with Aurora playing,
As he met her once a-Maying,
There, on Beds of Violets blue,
And fresh-blown Roses washed in dew,
Filled her with thee, a daughter fair,
So buxom, blithe, and debonair.
   Haste thee, Nymph, and bring with thee
Jest and youthful Jollity,

Quips and Cranks, and wanton Wiles,
Nods, and Becks, and Wreathèd Smiles,
Such as hang on Hebe's cheek,
And love to live in dimple sleek;
Sport that wrinkled Care derides,
And Laughter holding both his sides.
Come, and trip it as ye go
On the light fantastic toe,
And in thy right hand lead with thee,
The Mountain Nymph, sweet Liberty;
And if I give thee honor due,
Mirth, admit me of thy crew
To live with her, and live with thee,
In unreprovèd pleasures free;
To hear the Lark begin his flight,
And, singing, startle the dull night,
From his watch-tower in the skies,
Till the dappled dawn doth rise;
Then to come in spite of sorrow,
And at my window bid good-morrow,
Through the Sweet-Briar, or the Vine,
Or the twisted Eglantine.
While the Cock, with lively din,
Scatters the rear of darkness thin,
And to the stack, or the Barn-door,
Stoutly struts his Dames before,
Oft listening how the Hounds and horn
Clearly rouse the slumbering morn,
From the side of some Hoar Hill,
Through the high wood echoing shrill.
Some time walking not unseen
By Hedge-row Elms, on Hillocks green,
Right against the Eastern gate,
Where the great Sun begins his state,
Robed in flames, and Amber light,
The clouds in thousand Liveries dight.
While the Plowman, near at hand,

Whistles o'er the Furrowed Land,
And the Milkmaid singeth blithe,
And the Mower whets his scythe,
And every Shepherd tells his tale
Under the Hawthorn in the dale.
Straight mine eye hath caught new pleasures
Whilst the Landscape round it measures,
Russet Lawns, and Fallows Gray,
Where the nibbling flocks do stray,
Mountains on whose barren breast
The laboring clouds do often rest:
Meadows trim with Daisies pied,
Shallow Brooks, and Rivers wide.
Towers, and Battlements it sees
Bosomed high in tufted Trees,
Where perhaps some beauty lies,
The Cynosure of neighboring eyes.
Hard by a Cottage chimney smokes,
From betwixt two aged Oaks,
Where Corydon and Thyris met,
Are at their savory dinner set
Of Herbs, and other Country Messes,
Which the neat-handed Phillis dresses;
And then in haste her Bower she leaves,
With Thestylis to bind the Sheaves;
Or, if the earlier season lead,
To the tanned Haycock in the Mead.
Sometimes with secure delight
The upland Hamlets will invite,
When the merry Bells ring round,
And the jocund rebecks sound
To many a youth, and many a maid,
Dancing in the Chequered shade;
And young and old come forth to play
On a Sunshine Holyday,
Till the live-long day-light fail;
Then to the Spicy Nut-brown Ale,

[51]

With stories told of many a feat,
How Faery Mab the junkets eat.
She was pinched, and pulled she said;
And he, by Friar's Lantern led,
Tells how the drudging Goblin sweat,
To earn his Cream-bowl duly set,
When in one night, ere glimpse of morn,
His shadowy Flail hath threshed the Corn
That ten day-laborers could not end,
Then lies him down, the lubber fiend,
And stretched out all the Chimney's length,
Basks at the fire his hairy strength;
And Crop-full out of doors he flings,
Ere the first Cock his Matin rings.
Thus done the Tales, to bed they creep,
By whispering Winds soon lulled asleep.
    Towered Cities please us then,
And the busy hum of men,
Where throngs of Knights and Barons bold,
In weeds of Peace high triumphs hold,
With store of Ladies, whose bright eyes
Rain influence, and judge the prize
Of Wit, or Arms, while both contend
To win her Grace, whom all commend.
There let Hymen oft appear
In Saffron robe, with Taper clear,
And pomp, and feast, and revelry,
With mask, and antique Pageantry,
Such sights as youthful Poets dream
On Summer eves by haunted stream.
Then to the well-trod stage anon,
If Jonson's learnèd Sock be on,
Or sweetest Shakespeare, Fancy's child,
Warble his native Wood-notes wild;
And ever, against eating Cares,
Lap me in soft Lydian Airs,
Married to immortal verse

Such as the meeting soul may pierce
In notes, with many a winding bout
Of linkèd sweetness long drawn out,
With wanton heed, and giddy cunning,
The melting voice through mazes running;
Untwisting all the chains that tie
The hidden soul of harmony;
That Orpheus' self may heave his head
From golden slumber on a bed
Of heaped Elysian flowers, and hear
Such strains as would have won the ear
Of Pluto, to have quite set free
His half-regained Eurydice.
These delights, if thou canst give,
Mirth, with thee I mean to live.

Illustrations for

L'ALLEGRO

MIRTH AND HER COMPANIONS

These personifications are all brought together in the First design Surrounding the Principal Figure which is Mirth herself.

[56]

Mirth. Allegro

1 Heart easing Mirth.
Haste thee Nymph & bring with thee
Jest & Youthful Jollity
Quips & Cranks & Wanton Wiles
Nods & Becks & wreathed Smiles
Sport that wrinkled Care derides
And Laughter holding both his Sides
Come & trip it as you go
On the light phantastic toe
And in thy right hand lead with thee
The Mountain Nymph Sweet Liberty

These Personifications are all brought
together in the First Design. Surrounding
the Principal Figure which is Mirth
herself

Mirth and Her Companions

NIGHT STARTLED BY THE LARK

The Lark is an Angel on the Wing. Dull Night starts from his Watch Tower on a Cloud. The Dawn with her Dappled Horses arises above the Earth. The Earth beneath awakes at the Lark's Voice.

2 To hear the Lark begin his flight
And singing startle the dull Night
From his Watch Tower in the Skies
Till the dappled Dawn does rise

The Lark is an Angel on the Wing
Dull Night starts from his Watch Tower
on a Cloud. The Dawn with her
dappled Horses, arises above the Earth
The Earth beneath awakes at the
Larks Voice

Night Startled by the Lark

THE GREAT SUN

The Great Sun is represented clothed in Flames, Surrounded by the Clouds in
in their Liveries, in their various Offices at the Eastern Gate; beneath, in Small
Figures, Milton walking by Elms on Hillocks green, The Plowman, The
Milkmaid, The Mower whetting his Scythe, and The Shepherd and his Lass
under a Hawthorn in the Dale.

[64]

3 Sometime walking not unseen
By hedge row Elms on Hillocks green
Right against the Eastern Gate
When the Great Sun begins his state
Robed in Flames & amber Light
The Clouds in thousand Liveries dight
While the Plowman near at hand
Whistles o'er the Furrow'd Land
And the Milkmaid singeth blithe
And the Mower whets his Scythe
And every Shepherd tells his Tale
Under the Hawthorn in the dale

The Great Sun is represented clothed in
Flames Surrounded by the Clouds in their
Liveries. in their various Offices at the
Eastern Gate. beneath in Small Figures
Milton walking by Elms on Hillocks green
The Plowman. The Milkmaid The Mower
whetting his Scythe. & the Shepherd & his
Lass under a Hawthorn in the dale

The Great Sun

THE SUNSHINE HOLIDAY

In this design is Introduced,

                Mountains on whose barren breast
                The labouring Clouds do often rest.

Mountains, Clouds, Rivers, Trees appear Humanized on the Sunshine Holiday. The Church Steeple with its merry bells. The Clouds arise from the bosoms of Mountains, While Two Angels sound their Trumpets in the Heavens to announce the Sunshine Holiday.

[68]

4 Sometimes with secure delight
The upland Hamlets will invite
When the merry Bells ring round
And the jocund Rebecks sound
To many a youth & many a Maid
Dancing in the chequerd Shade
And Young & Old come forth to play
On a Sunshine Holiday

In this design is Introduced
Mountains on whose barren breast
The labring Clouds do often rest
Mountains Clouds Rivers Trees appear
Humanized on the Sunshine Holiday. The
Church Steeple with its merry bells, The
Clouds arise from the bosom of Mountains,
While Two Angels Sound their Trumpets
in the Heavens to announce the Sunshine
Holiday

The Sunshine Holiday

THE STORIES OF CORYDON AND THYRSIS

The Goblin crop full flings out of doors from his Laborious task dropping his Flail & Cream bowl, yawning & stretching, vanishes into the Sky, in which is seen Queen Mab Eating the Junkets. The Sports of the Fairies are seen thro' the Cottage where "She" lays in Bed 'pinch'd & pull'd' by Fairies as they dance on the Bed, the Ceiling & the Floor, & a Ghost pulls the Bed Clothes at her Feet. "He" is seen following the Friar's Lantern towards the Convent.

5 Then to the Spicy Nut brown Ale
With Stories told of many a Treat
How Fairy Mab the Junkets eat
She was pinch'd & pull'd she said
And he by Friars Lantern led
Tells how the Drudging Goblin sweat
To earn his Cream Bowl duly set
When in one Night e'er glimpse of Morn
His Shadowy Flail had thresh'd the Corn
That ten day Labourers could not end
Then crop-full out of door he flings
E'er the first Cock his Matin rings

The Goblin crop full flings out of doors
from his Laborious task dropping his Flail
& Cream bowl yawning & stretching vanishes
into the Sky, in which is seen Queen Mab
Eating the Junkets. The Sports of the Fairies
are seen thro' the Cottage where "She" lays
in Bed pinch'd & pull'd "by Fairies as they Dance
on the Bed the Cieling & the Floor & a Ghost
pulls the Bed Clothes at her Feet. "He" is seen
following the Friars Lantern towards the Concourse

The Stories of Corydon and Thyrsis

THE YOUNG POET'S DREAM

The Youthful Poet, sleeping on a bank by the Haunted Stream by Sun Set, sees in his dream the more bright Sun of Imagination under the auspices of Shakespeare & Johnson [Jonson], in which is Hymen at a Marriage & the Antique Pageantry attending it.

[76]

6 There let Hymen oft appear
In Saffron Robe with Taper clear
With Mask & antique Pageantry
Such sights as youthful Poets dream
On Summer's Eve by haunted Stream
Then to the well trod Stage anon
If Johnsons learned Sock be on
Or sweetest Shakespeare Fancys Child
Warble his native woodnotes wild

The youthful Poet sleeping on a bank
by the haunted Stream by Sun set
sees in his Dream the more bright Sun
of Sun of Imagination under the auspices
of Shakespeare & Johnson. in which is
Hymen at a Marriage & the Antique
Pageantry attending it

The Young Poet's Dream

IL PENSEROSO

by John Milton

HENCE vain deluding Joys,
  The brood of Folly without father bred!
  How little you bestead,
 Or fill the fixèd mind with all your toys;
Dwell in some idle brain,
  And fancies fond with gaudy shapes possess,
As thick and numberless
  As the gay motes that people the sun-beams,
Or likest hovering dreams
  The fickle Pensioners of Morpheus' train.
But hail, thou Goddess, sage and holy,
Hail, divinest Melancholy!
Whose Saintly visage is too bright
To hit the sense of human sight;
And therefore to our weaker view,
O'er-laid with black, staid Wisdom's hue.
Black, but such as in esteem,
Prince Memnon's sister might beseem,
Or that Starred Ethiope Queen that strove
To set her beauty's praise above
The Sea Nymphs, and their powers offended.
Yet thou art higher far descended:
Thee bright-haired Vesta long of yore,
To solitary Saturn bore;
His daughter she (in Saturn's reign,
Such mixture was not held a stain).
Oft in glimmering Bowers, and glades
He met her, and in secret shades

[81]

Of woody Ida's inmost grove,
Whilst yet there was no fear of Jove.
Come, pensive Nun, devout and pure,
Sober, steadfast, and demure,
All in a robe of darkest grain,
Flowing with majestic train,
And sable stole of Cypress Lawn,
Over thy decent shoulders drawn.
Come, but keep thy wonted state,
With even step, and musing gait,
And looks commercing with the skies,
Thy rapt soul sitting in thine eyes:
There, held in holy passion still,
Forget thy self to Marble, till
With a sad Leaden downward cast,
Thou fix them on the earth as fast.
And join with thee calm Peace, and Quiet,
Spare Fast, that oft with gods doth diet,
And hears the Muses in a ring,
Aye round about Jove's Altar sing.
And add to these retired Leisure,
That in trim Gardens takes his pleasure;
But first, and chiefest, with thee bring,
Him that yon soars on golden wing,
Guiding the fiery-wheeled throne,
The Cherub Contemplation,
And the mute Silence hist along,
'Less Philomel will deign a Song,
In her sweetest, saddest plight,
Smoothing the rugged brow of Night,
While Cynthia checks her Dragon yoke,
Gently o'er th' accustomed Oak;
Sweet Bird, that shunn'st the noise of folly,
Most musical, most melancholy!
Thee, Chauntress, oft the Woods among,
I woo to hear thy even-song;
And missing thee, I walk unseen

On the dry smooth-shaven Green,
To behold the wandering Moon,
Riding near her highest noon,
Like one that had been led astray
Through the Heaven's wide pathless way;
And oft, as if her head she bowed,
Stooping through a fleecy cloud.
Oft on a Plat of rising ground,
I hear the far-off Curfew sound,
Over some wide-watered shore,
Swinging slow with sullen roar;
Or if the Air will not permit,
Some still removèd place will fit,
Where glowing Embers through the room
Teach light to counterfeit a gloom,
Far from all resort of mirth,
Save the Cricket on the hearth,
Or the Bellman's drowsy charm,
To bless the doors from nightly harm:
Or let my Lamp, at midnight hour,
Be seen in some high lonely Tower,
Where I may oft out-watch the Bear,
With thrice great Hermes, or unsphere
The spirit of Plato to unfold
What Worlds, or what vast Regions hold
The immortal mind that hath forsook
Her mansion in this fleshly nook:
And of those Daemons that are found
In fire, air, flood, or under ground,
Whose power hath a true consent
With Planet, or with Element.
Some time let Gorgeous Tragedy
In Sceptered Pall come sweeping by,
Presenting Thebes, or Pelops' line,
Or the tale of Troy divine,
Or what (though rare) of later age,
Ennoblèd hath the Buskined stage.

But, O sad Virgin, that thy power
Might raise Musaeus from his bower,
Or bid the soul of Orpheus sing
Such notes as, warbled to the string,
Drew Iron tears down Pluto's cheek,
And made Hell grant what Love did seek.
Or call up him that left half told
The story of Cambuscan bold,
Of Camball, and of Algarsife,
And who had Canace to wife,
That owned the virtuous Ring and Glass,
And of the wondrous Horse of Brass,
On which the Tartar King did ride;
And if aught else great Bards beside,
In sage and solemn tunes have sung,
Of Tourneys and of Trophies hung;
Of Forest, and enchantments drear,
Where more is meant than meets the ear.
Thus, Night, oft see me in thy pale career,
Till civil-suited Morn appear,
Not tricked and frounced as she was wont,
With the Attic Boy to hunt,
But Kerchiefed in a comely Cloud,
While rocking Winds are Piping loud,
Or ushered with a shower still,
When the gust hath blown his fill,
Ending on the rustling Leaves,
With minute-drops from off the Eaves.
And when the Sun begins to fling
His flaring beams, me, Goddess, bring
To archèd walks of twilight groves,
And shadows brown, that Sylvan loves,
Of Pine, or monumental Oak,
Where the rude Ax with heavèd stroke,
Was never heard the Nymphs to daunt,
Or fright them from their hallowed haunt.
There in close covert by some Brook,

Where no profaner eye may look,
Hide me from Day's garish eye,
While the Bee with Honied thigh,
That at her flowery work doth sing,
And the Waters murmuring
With such consort as they keep,
Entice the dewy-feathered Sleep;
And let some strange mysterious dream,
Wave at his Wings, in Airy stream
Of lively portraiture displayed,
Softly on my eye-lids laid.
And as I wake, sweet music breathe
Above, about, or underneath,
Sent by some Spirit to mortals good,
Or th' unseen Genius of the Wood.
   But let my due feet never fail,
To walk the studious Cloister's pale,
And love the high embowèd Roof,
With antique Pillars massy proof.
And storied Windows richly dight,
Casting a dim religious light.
There let the pealing Organ blow,
To the full voiced choir below,
In Service high, and Anthems clear,
As may with sweetness, through mine ear,
Dissolve me into ecstasies,
And bring all Heaven before mine eyes.
And may at last my weary age
Find out the peaceful hermitage,
The Hairy Gown and Mossy Cell,
Where I may sit and rightly spell
Of every Star that Heaven doth shew,
And every Herb that sips the dew;
Till old experience do attain
To something like Prophetic strain.
These pleasures, Melancholy, give,
And I with thee will choose to live.

Illustrations for

IL PENSEROSO

MELANCHOLY AND HER COMPANIONS

These Personifications are all brought together in this design, surrounding the Principal Figure Who is Melancholy Herself.

Melancholy. Penservoso

7 Come pensive Nun devout & pure
   Sober stedfast & demure
   All in Robe of darkest grain
   Flowing with magestic train
   Come but keep thy wonted state
   With even step & musing gait
   And looks commercing with the Skies

   And join with thee calm Peace & Quiet
   Spare Fast who oft with Gods doth diet
   And hear the Muses in a ring
   Ay. round about Joves altar sing
   And add to these retired Leisure
   Who in trim Gardens takes his pleasure
   But first & chiefest with thee bring
   Him who yon soars on golden Wing
   Guiding the fiery wheeled Throne
   The Cherub Contemplation

   Less Philomel will deign a song
   In her sweetest saddest plight
   Smoothing the rugged Brow of Night
   While Cynthia checks her Dragon yoke
   Gently o'er the accustomed Oak

These Personifications are all brought together in
this design Surrounding the Principal figure who is
        Melancholy herself

Melancholy and Her Companions

MILTON'S VISION OF THE MOON

Milton in his character of a Student at Cambridge, Sees the Moon terrified as one led astray in the midst of her path thro heaven. The distant Steeple seen across a wide water indicates the sound of the Curfew Bell.

8 To behold the wandring Moon
Riding near her highest Noon
Like one that has been led astray
Thro the heavens wide pathless way
And oft as if her head she bowd
Stooping thro' a fleecy Cloud
Oft on a plat of rising ground
I hear the far off Curfew sound
Over some wide waterd shore
Swinging slow with sullen war
Mellom in his Character of a Student
at Cambridge sees the Moon terrified
as one led astray in the midst of her
path thro heaven. The distant Steeple
seen across a wide water indicates
the Sound of the Curfew Bell

Milton's Vision of the Moon

MILTON AND THE SPIRIT OF PLATO

The Spirit of Plato unfolds his Worlds to Milton in Contemplation. The Three Destinies sit on the Circles of Plato's Heavens, weaving the Thread of Mortal Life; these Heavens are Venus, Jupiter & Mars. Hermes flies before as attending on the Heaven of Jupiter; the Great Bear is seen in the sky beneath Hermes & the Spirits of Fire, Air, Water & Earth Surround Milton's Chair.

[96]

9 Where I may oft outwatch the Bear
With thrice great Hermes or unsphear
The Spirit of Plato to unfold
What Worlds or what vast regions hold
The Immortal Mind that has forsook
Its Mansion in this fleshly nook
And of those Spirits that are found
In Fire. Air. Flood. & Underground

The Spirit of Plato unfolds his Worlds
to Milton in Contemplation. The Three
Destinies sit on the Circles of Plato's
Heavens weaving the Thread of Mortal
Life these Heavens are Venus Jupiter
& Mars. Hermes flies before as attending
on the Heaven of Jupiter the Great Bear
is seen in the Sky beneath Hermes &
The Spirit of Fire. Air. Water & Earth
Surround Miltons Chair

Milton and the Spirit of Plato

MILTON LED BY MELANCHOLY

Milton led by Melancholy into the Groves away from the Sun's flaming
Beams, who is seen in the Heavens throwing his darts & flames of fire. The
Spirits of the Trees on each side are seen under the domination of Insects
raised by the Sun's heat.

[100]

10   And when the Sun begins to fling
His flaring Beams, me Goddess bring
To arched walks of twilight Groves,
And Shadows brown that Sylvan loves
Milton led by Melancholy into the Groves
away from the Suns flaring Beams who is
seen in the Heavens throwing his darts &
& flames of fire The Spirits of the Trees
on each Side are seen under the Domina
tion of Insects raised by the Suns heat

Milton Led by Melancholy

MILTON'S DREAM

Milton Sleeping on a Bank; Sleep descending, with a strange, Mysterious dream upon his Wings, of Scrolls & Nets & Webs, unfolded by Spirits in the Air & in the Brook. Around Milton are Six Spirits or Fairies, hovering on the air, with Instruments of Music.

[104]

11 There in close Covert by some Brook
Where no profaner Eye may look
With such Concert as they keep
Entice the dewy feather'd Sleep
And let some strange mysterious Dream
Wave on his Wings in airy stream
Of lively portraiture display'd.
On my sleeping eyelids laid
And as I wake sweet Music breathe
Above; about: or underneath
Sent by some spirit to Mortals good
Or the unseen Genius of the Wood

Milton sleeping on a Bank. Sleep
descending with a strange Mysterious
Dream upon his Wings of Scrolls &
Nets & Webs unfolded by Spirits in the
Air & in the Brook around Milton
are Six Spirits or Fairies hovering on the
air with Instruments of Music

Milton's Dream

THE PEACEFUL HERMITAGE

Milton in his Old Age sitting in his "Mossy Cell," Contemplating the Constellations, surrounded by the Spirits of the Herbs & Flowers, bursts forth into a rapturous Prophetic Strain.

12 And may at last my weary Age
Find out the peaceful Hermitage
The hairy Gown the mossy Cell
Where I may sit & rightly spell
Of every Star that heaven doth shew
And every Herb that sips the dew
Till old Experience do attain
To somewhat like Prophetic Strain

Milton in his Old Age sitting in his
Mossy Cell Contemplating the Constellations. Surrounded by the Spirits of the
Herbs & Flowers. bursts forth into a
rapturous Prophetic Strain

The Peaceful Hermitage

NOTES ON THE POEMS

L'Allegro

AURORA—Early morning. The Goddess Aurora sets out before the sun and is the pioneer of his rising

BACCHUS—God of wine

CEREBRUS—A three-headed dog in Roman mythology which kept the entrance to the infernal regions

CORYDON—A shepherd

ELYSIAN—Delightful

EUPHROSYNE—One of the three graces in classical mythology

EURYDICE—Wife of Orpheus

HEBE—Goddess of youth—wife of Hercules

HYMEN—Goddess of marriage

JOCUND—Merry

JONSON—The English dramatist, Ben Jonson, was known for his style and rigid observance of the theoretic principles in writing. Best known for his comedy, *Everyman In His Humor*

LYDIAN AIRS—The Lydian mode was one of the four modes of ancient classical music and was appropriate to pathos

MAB—Queen of the fairies

ORPHEUS—A poet who could move even inanimate things by his music. He went to the infernal regions to retrieve his wife after her death and so charmed Pluto with his music that she was released on the condition that Orpheus should not look back until they reached the earth. At the last instant before the exit from the infernal regions, Orpheus turned around whereupon Eurydice vanished

PHILLIS—A maiden

REBECK—A stringed instrument, progenitor of the viol

SOCK—A lowheeled, light shoe worn by actors in comedies

"If Jonson's learned sock be on": to wit, if comedy is being played

STYGIAN CAVE—Refers to the river of Hate called Styx, which flowed around the infernal regions

THESTYLIS—Poetic name for a rustic maiden

THYRSIS—A rustic

VENUS—Goddess of love and beauty

ZEPHRY—The west wind

Il Penseroso

ATTIC BOY—Cephalus, a hunter beloved by Aurora

BEAR—A constellation

BUSKIN—A half boot worn by Greek tragic actors to raise their stature

CAMBUSCAN—A king in Tartary who is featured in the unfinished *Squire's Tale* of Chaucer. He had two sons Cambalo and Algarsife and a daughter Canace. To Cambuscan on his daughter's birthday, the King of Arabia sent a brass horse which was supposed to be able to carry its rider to any spot on the earth between the hours of sunrise and sunset. It was necessary only for the rider to whisper in the ear of the horse the name of the desired destination, then mount him, and turn a pin in his ear. On the arrival at the end of the journey, the rider had to turn another pin, upon which the horse immediately descended out of the clouds

CYNTHIA—The moon

HERMES—Another name for Mercury who was a messenger

JOVE—Same as Jupiter, who was identified with Zeus, chief of the Olympian Gods

MEMNON—Ethiopian prince slain in defense of his uncle Priam in the Trojan War

MORPHEUS—God of dreams

ORPHEUS—A poet who could move even inanimate things by his music. He went to the infernal regions to retrieve his wife after her death and so charmed Pluto with his music that she was released on the condition that Orpheus should not look back until they reached the earth. At the last instant before the exit from the infernal regions Orpheus turned around whereupon Eurydice vanished

PHILOMELA—Daughter of Pandion, King of Attica. According to Greek legend Tereus, the King of Thrace brought Philomela to visit his wife who was her sister; on the journey he dishonored her and then cut out her tongue that she might not reveal his conduct. Tereus told his wife that Philomela was dead. The gods changed all three into birds; Tereus into a hawk, his wife into a swallow, and Philomela into a nightingale, a bird which poets still call Philomel

PLATO—Famous Greek philosopher, disciple of Socrates, author of *The Republic* and of *The Symposium*—a dialogue on ideal love which has given rise to the term Platonic love

PELOPS—Son of Tantalus. Legend has it he was cut to pieces and served as food to the Gods; "Pelops' line" means Greek

SATURN—Roman deity who devoured all his children except Jupiter (air), Neptune (water) and Pluto (the grave), being three which time could not consume

THEBES—Town in upper Egypt, hence Egyptian

VESTA—Virgin goddess of the hearth and custodian of the sacred fire brought by Aeneas from Troy

PARTIAL LIST OF BLAKE'S BOOKS
IN ORDER OF PUBLICATION

Poetical Sketches	1787
There is no Natural Religion	1789
Tiriel	1789
Songs of Innocence	1789
The Book of Thel	1789
The Marriage of Heaven and Hell	1790
The French Revolution	1791
Rossetti Manuscript	1793
Visions of the Daughters of Albion	1793
America, A Prophecy	1793
For Children: The Gates of Paradise	1793
Songs of Innocence and Experience	1794
Europe, A Prophecy	1794
The First Book of Urizen	1794
The Book of Ahania	1795
The Book of Los	1795
The Song of Los	1795
The Four Zoas	1804
Milton, A Poem	1808
Annotations to Sir Joshua Reynolds' Discourses	1808
A Descriptive Catalogue	1809
Jerusalem, The Emanation of the Giant Albion	1820

SELECTED BIBLIOGRAPHY

Binyon, Laurence. *William Blake Illustrations of the Book of Job: With a General Introduction.* London: Methuen & Co. 1906.

Binyon, Laurence. Geoffrey Holme, Ed. *The Drawings and Engravings of William Blake.* London: The Studio, Ltd. 1922.

Blackstone, Bernard. *English Blake.* Cambridge: Cambridge University Press. 1949.

Bruce, Harold Lawton. *William Blake in This World.* New York: Harcourt, Brace and Co. 1925.

Damon, S. Foster. *William Blake, His Philosophy and Symbols.* Boston: Houghton Mifflin and Co. 1924.

Ellis, Edwin J. *The Real Blake.* London: Chatto and Windus. 1897.

Garnett, Richard. *William Blake, Painter and Poet.* New York: Macmillan Co. 1895.

Gilchrist, Alexander. *Life of William Blake, "Pictor Ignotus."* Two Volumes. London: Macmillan Co. 1863.

Gilchrist, Alexander. *Life of William Blake With Selections from his Poems and Other Writings.* Two Volumes. London: Macmillan Co. 1880.

Kazin, Alfred, Editor and arranger. *The Portable Blake.* New York: Viking Press. 1946.

Keynes, Geoffrey. *John Milton: Poems in English, with Illustrations by William Blake.* Two Volumes, London: Nonesuch Press. 1926.

Keynes, Geoffrey, Editor. *The Writings of William Blake.* Three Volumes. London: Nonesuch Press. 1925.

Keynes, Geoffrey. *A Bibliography of William Blake.* New York: Grolier Club of New York. 1921.

Plowman, Max. *An Introduction to the Study of Blake.* London and Toronto: 1927.

Sampson, John. *The Poetical Works of William Blake.* Oxford: Clarendon Press. 1905.

Saurat, Denis. *Blake and Milton.* London: S. Nott. 1935.

Schorer, Mark. *William Blake, The Politics of Vision.* New York: Holt and Co. 1946.

de Sélincourt, Basil. *William Blake.* New York: Charles Scribner's Sons. 1909.

Sloss, D. J. and Wallis, J. P. R., Editors. *The Prophetic Writings of William Blake.* Oxford: Clarendon Press. 1926.

Story, Alfred T. *The Life of John Linnell.* Two Volumes. London: Richard Bentley and Son. 1892.

Story, Alfred T. *William Blake, His Life Character and Genius.* New York: Macmillan Co. 1893.

Swinburne, Charles. *William Blake, A Critical Essay.* London: Chatto and Windus. 1906.

Symons, Arthur. *William Blake.* New York: E. P. Dutton and Co. 1907.

Engraved and printed by The Beck Engraving Company

Designed by Lucia Howe